A TRIBUTE TO LOVE

HORROR DEATH AND THE CRUMBLING MIND

A BOOK OF MAGICK POEMS

DAVID WAR

A TRIBUTE TO LOVE HORROR DEATH AND THE CRUMBLING MIND

Author: DAVID WAR

Copyright © DAVID WAR (2023)

The right of DAVID WAR to be identified as author of this work has been asserted by the author in accordance with section 77 and 78 of the Copyright, Designs and Patents Act 1988.

First Published in 2023

ISBN 978-1-915996-95-4 (Paperback)
978-1-915996-96-1 (Hardback)
978-1-915996-97-8 (E-Book)

Cover Design and Book Layout by:
White Magic Studios
www.whitemagicstudios.co.uk

Published by:
Maple Publishers
Fairbourne Drive, Atterbury,
Milton Keynes,
MK10 9RG, UK
www.maplepublishers.com

A CIP catalogue record for this title is available from the British Library.

All rights reserved. No part of this book may be reproduced or translated by any form or by any means, electronic or mechanical, including photocopying, recording or by any information storage and retrieval system without written permission from the author.

The views expressed in this work are solely those of the author and do not necessarily reflect the views of the publisher, and the publisher hereby disclaims any responsibility for them.

THIS BOOK IS DEDICATED

TO

EDGAR ALLAN POE

THE MASTER OF

HORROR GOTHIC MACABRE

CRIME

BORN

ALAN JAMES FOULDS

1978 IRVINE SCOTLAND

DAVID WAR

CREATED 1994

FROM THE HEART OF

HEAVEN FROM THE

SOUL OF HELL

THIS BOOK IS DEDICATED

TO NADIA

MY BEST FRIEND

MUSE LOVE OF MY LIFE

MOTHER FIGURE PROTECTOR

DEDICATED TO THE MAGICK MIRRORS

SARAH JANE

ANN

SARAH

CAROLINE

EMMA

AVRIL

NAGOZI

DANYELA

JOANE

JOANE

JOANE

DEBBIE

TEREZA

JEZICA

LINDA

LAUNRA

A Tribute To Love Horror Death And The Crumbling Mind

ALLISON

JENET

SHARON

ANTIWINET

CARMEN

ANGEILA

CATHRIN

CAROL

JACQULIN

LARNA

FAY

NICKI

SHELLY

REMEMBER

DO WHAT THU WILT

SHALL BE THE WHOLE OF

THE LAW ITS MAGICK

II MAGICAL NUMBER SO ADD THE K

FAVORITE POET

LORD BYRON

ACTOR

KLAUS KINSKI

DIRECTOR

SAM PECKINPAH

MOVIE

COOL HAND LUKE

CLASSICAL

PAGANINI

WRITER

JACK KEROUAC

BAND

THE DOORS

SONG WRITER POET

BOB DYLAN

ART

VINCINT VAN GO

BLUES

LEAD BELLY

PUNK

PATTI SMITH

FOLK

WOODY GUTHRIE

JAZZ

MILES DAVIS

A Tribute To Love Horror Death And The Crumbling Mind

CLASSICAL

JACQUELINE DU PRÉ

ROCK 'N' ROLL BAND

MOTHERHEAD

COUNTRY

JOHNNY CASH

DEDICATED TO HAMMER HORROR AND THE ACTORS

CHRISTOPHER LEE

PETER CUSHING

VINCENT PRICE

1

DARK SECRETS

CALL THE SEEKER

INTO THE SOUL OF MADNESS I MUST

DIG DEEPER

2

A CELEBRATION OF LOVE AND PAIN AND BOTH KNOW MY NAME.

IT'S THE MONSTERS OF THE HUMAN CONDITION I HAVE NO WISH TO TAME.

HORROR FANS THE FLAME OF MY IMAGINATION OBSESSED BY THE SLOW PAINFUL DEATH CAN THERE BE A BETTER FASINATION. WICKED WOMAN TORTURED MAN ON A MOUNTAIN MADE OF THE MACABRE I STAND.

3

I MUST BECOME FRIENDS WITH WHAT THE GOOD PEOPLE FEAR THE MOST

TO THE PUREST FORM OF EVIL I AM A LOYAL HOST

A SOUL DESTROYER INSANE ASYLUM DISCIPLE A LIVING GHOST

4

FRIENDSHIP PURE AND TRUE NOT INTERESTED IN A ROOM WITH A VIEW.

SORRY I NEVER PUT MY ARMS AROUND YOU WHEN THE DARKNESS VISITED IT WAS A CONCRETE DECISION NOTHING TO DO WITH BEING CONFUSED.

I'M MADE OF SAND YOU ARE MADE OF GOLD NEVER SHALL I LOVE.

IN MY HEART ITS FEAR I HOLD.

A TRIBUTE TO THE MAGICK 4

1

A TRIBUTE TO THE CRUMBLING MIND
IT'S ONLY WHAT THE DARKNESS
HIDES I WANT TO FIND
SWEET JOURNEY TO THE
JOYESS END GOTHIC
PARADISE
THE PIT OF IMAGINATION
MY SOUL DESCENDS

2

DARK FORCES FUEL MY
IMAGINATION FOR HELL
IS MY FINAL DESTINATION

3

THE UNHOLY STORM THAT
RAGES FROM DUST TILL
DAWN A CONSTANT
BATTLE BETWEEN RIGHT AND
WRONG THE SIDE OF EVIL
I BELONG ON ME THE LIGHT OF LOVE
HAS NEVER SHAWN.

4

SEND ME LOVE TO SOFTEN THE PAIN
FOR THE DEVILS POET LOVE IS A LOOSENING
GAME

5

THE DEVILS POET SHALL
WHIP THE GODDESS OF LOVE
THE DEMONS FROM
BELOW SHALL DESTROY THE ANGELS
FROM ABOVE

6

FROM THE WAR OF LOVE
I SHALL NOT RETURN
ON A FIRE MADE OF
REGRETS MY BODY SHALL
BURN

7

WILDTIMES IS WHAT I DEMAND

I SHALL FEAST ON EXCESS IN

EVERY EXOTIC LAND

FOR IT'S THE GHOSTS OF

PLEASURE I COMMAND

ON MY DEATHBED NO TRUE

LOVE HOLDS MY HAND

8

DEATH IS THE REASON

I SWEAT AND SLAVE

LOVE IS A CREATURE MADE

OF CLAY

JOURNEY OF DESPAIR IS

THE ONLY WAY

9

DREAMS ABOUT THE INSANE

I LOOK IN THE MIRROR

I SEE SOMEONE IN PAIN

THE ENDLESS HIGHWAY

KEEPER OF THE FLAME

10

WICKED LOVE I LOVE

TO CHASE

PURE EVIL I EMBRACE

WITH NO REGRETS I FALL

FROM GRACE

11

I'M YOUR LOYAL SLAVE

YOUR LOYAL GHOST FROM

BEYOND THE GRAVE

12

POEMS WRITTEN IN MY
MUSES BLOOD
GOTHIC BONES BLOCK THE
RIVER OF LOVE

13

CREATIVITY STOLEN FROM
THE DEAD
A THOUSAND CORPS BRIDES
INSIDE MY HEAD
I ABANDON LOVE FOR
TORTURE INSTEAD

14

DEATH STRANGLES THE

POETS MIND

A FOLLOWER OF PAIN

I'M A SLAVE TO THE

GRIND

15

FROM BIRTH LOVE HAS HAD

A GRAVE

FROM DEATH MY CREATIVITY IS MADE

FROM A DOOMED FUTURE

I DON'T WANT TO BE

SAVED

16

TWISTED MIND THE PLACE
WHERE MADNESS SHINES
AND ARE COMMITTED THE
UNHOLIEST OF CRIMES
ALL THAT WORSHIPS HELL
I NEED TO FIND

17

MADNESS INFECTS THE
FRAGILE MIND LOVE IS
IN THE DARK
IN MY HEART ITS
ONLY HATE YOU WILL
FIND

18

LOVE IS MURDERED BY HATE
A HAPPY ENDING HAS COME TOO LATE
A PAINFUL DEATH ALL
ALONE I WAIT

19

LOVE I MUST DESTROY
ONLY DEATH BRINGS ME
JOY

20

WINTER PAIN
SUICIDE JUST A GAME
NEVER TO SEE SUMMERS
FLAME

21

NO LOVE

NO HEAVEN

JUST LOVE AND

OBLIVION

22

MADNESS STAYS AND

OBEYS

LOVE LEAVES AND

BETRAYS

23

A WARM WELCOME TO

DEATH

LOVE IS HELL ON EARTH

THE MASTERS OF

DARKNESS I WORSHIP

AND SERVE

24

DAYS FILLED WITH PAIN AND SORROW

LOST MY FAITH IN TOMORROW

25

LOVE HAS NEVER BEEN

A FRIEND ON DEATH I CAN ONLY DEPEND

SELF-INFLICTED PAIN

OBSESSED BY THE END

26

DEATH BLOOMS LIKE A

SUMMER FLOWER

IN WINTER LOVE DIES

WITH EACH SMILING

HOUR

27

MY MIND DECAYING

AND LOVE BETRAYING

THE VOICES OF MADNESS

I AM OBEYING

28

LOVE TO SEE YOUR BLOOD

CALLING OUT FOR DEATH

I NEED TO WITNESS YOUR TERRIFIED EACH

DYING BREATH

29

A PAINFUL DEATH I

SHALL DELIVER

A CURSE ON LOVE

LASTING FOREVER

30

HARDTIMES WATCHING LOVE

FROM THE SIDELINES

IT'S SIN THAT GETS

ME THROUGH THE NIGHT TIME

LONELINESS IS THE ONLY

THING THAT'S ONLY TRULY

MINE

31

HANGING OUT IN PLACES I DON'T BELONG
NOT INTERESTED IN FIXING ALL THE
THINGS I'VE DONE WRONG.
THE DEVIL WRITES THE WORDS
BUT IT'S ME WHO SINGS
THE SONG.
FOR THOSE WHO LOVE WILL GET
NO SHELTER FROM THE STORM

32

HAPPY TO LET THE DARKEST
OF DEMONS VISIT MY
DREAMS.
FOR ME THERE WILL BE
NO HOLY SCREAMS

33

THE SHOCKING TRUTH
THE TORTURE CHAMBER
WAS THE PLAYGROUND OF
MY YOUTH

34

DEATH REPLACES LOVE
AND SHADOWS ARE MY
FRIENDS
JUST ME AND MADNESS
WAITING FOR THE END

35

I'M THE MASTER OF THE
MACABRE INTO YOUR
HEART ITS TERROR
I STAB

36

OF DEATH I'M DREAMING

LOVE IS BLEEDING

UNHAPPINESS IS ALL I

BELIEVE IN

37

I HAVE A TALENT FOR

HURTING PEOPLE AND LETTING

THEM DOWN

I'M THE MAKER OF

DISAPPOINTMENT

IN A RIVER OF PAIN

I SHALL DROWN

38

DEATH IS LOVE AND

LOVE IS PAIN

TORTURED HEART

ONLY MY SELF TO BLAME

39

TO DEATH I CONFESS

IN DEATH I INVEST

EVERYDAY DEATH IS A

TEST

DEATH STANDS OUT FROM

THE BEST

40
POEM FOR NADIA

IVE JUST LOVE YOU LIKE A

SHADOW LOVES THE NIGHT

IVE JUST LOVE YOU THEN

I CAN BE HATEFUL AS I LIKE

IVE JUST LOVE YOU LIKE A

FLOWER LOVES THE SUN

IVE JUST LOVE YOU

THEN I CAN UNDO ALL

THE GOOD I'VE DONE

41

LOVE MEANS NOTHING TO
ME
HOPES AND DREAMS COMMIT
SUICIDE UNLIKE ME.
I LOVE TO SUFFER
FROM THE CLUTCHES OF
DEATH I DON'T WANT
TO BE SET FREE

42

DEATH GETS A STANDING
OVATION
THE SADNESS READY FOR
INVASION
THE BEST WAY TO
KEEP OUT LOVE IS MY
ONLY FRUSTRATION

43

LOVE QUALIFIES FOR

ASSIGNATION

DEATH DOMINATES MY

IMAGINATION

44

I'M THE MONSTER POET

A PRISONER OF THE

INSANE

AND LOVE IS MY BALL

AND CHAIN

45

NO NEED TO HIDE

GOING TO FEED YOU PAIN

SO OPEN UP WIDE

46

IT'S LIKE I HAVE TO
DESTROY LOVE BEFORE
IT DESTROYS ME
I'M EVIL AND I'M SURE
YOU ALL AGREE

47

WELCOME TO THE DARK
SCENE
IT'S ABOUT DEATH I
DREAM
I CAN HEAR LOVE
SCREAM

48

THE PRIEST HE MADE

ME GO BLIND

THE POET HE BLEW MY MIND

BEING HOMELESS TURNED ME

ONTO CRIME

49

POEM FOR NADIA

MENTAL STATE

YOU WILL SURVIVE BUT

FOR ME IT'S TOO LATE

YOU'RE ADDICTED TO LOVE

I'M ADDICTED TO HATE

HEAVEN BENT OUT OF SHAPE

GO ALONE, FOR ME IT'S TOO LATE

50

BROKEN HEART CRYING

ALONE IN THE DARK

MISTAKES MADE AT

THE START

BUT AT THE END

NOTHING COULD TEAR US

APART

51

THIS TOWN MEANS NOTHING

TO ME THIS GIRIL DOES

NOTHING FOR ME

TO EVERYONE EVERYTHING I

HAVE TO BE

52

A STRUGGLE BEING ME

TO LOVE OR TO BE FREE

53

MY SOUL NEEDS PROTECTION

SO AFRAID OF REJECTION

AND SO THAT'S WHY ME

AND DEATH HAVE A

CONNECTION

54

THE WORD LOVE WRITTEN

IN BLOOD

DAM MADE BY GOD

CAN'T HOLD BACK

THE DEVIL'S FLOOD

55

LOVE I'M OUT TO DESTROY

I'M A MURDERER

AND WHEN I COUNT THE DEAD

BODIES

IT FILLS MY HEART WITH JOY

56

AN EARLY DEATH HAS BEEN

A CONSTANT SHADOW

THE CANYON OF LOVE

AND HOPE HAS ALWAYS

BEEN NARROW

57

FRIGHTENED OF LOVE

EXCESS AND SIN

I CAN'T GET ENGOUGH

58

JUST AS MUCH HELL ABOVE

AS THERE IS BELOW

MY WOMEN DON'T SAY MUCH

BUT SHE PUTS ON A GOOD

SHOW

59

NO GOING BACK

FROM NOW ON LOVE IS UNDER

ATTACK

FOR YOU THE SKY IS BLUE

FOR ME IT'S BLACK

60

LOVE IS AFRAID TO ENTER MY
HEART
HAPPINESS IS A FALSE START
HELL ENTERS
HEAVEN DEPARTS

61

MY IMAGINATION KEEPS
THE EDGE OF BEING ALONE
I KEEP LOVE AWAY
I'VE GOT A HEART OF
STONE

62

DEATH IS THE REASON

LOVE IS OUT OF SEASON

AND WHY I'M ALWAYS

DISSAPPEARING

63

TO LOVE I'M BLIND

TO YOU I'M UNKIND

I DESTROY ALL THE GOOD

I FIND

64

IN YOUR HEART I DON'T

BELONG

65

LOVE IS A HEAVY LOAD AND I'M
NOT THAT STRONG
AND THERE'S SO MUCH I DID
WRONG
NOT GOING TO SHED ANY
TEARS WHEN I'M GONE

66

IVE I DON'T TRY
THEN I'M GOING TO DIE
STRANGERS ASK WHY
AND FRIENDS THEY CRY

67

YOU ALL MUST DIE

AND ONLY THE DEVIL KNOWS

WHY

HIDE LOVE AWAY AND

KEEP DEATH ON DISPLAY

68

DOWN AND OUT

ANALYZING WHAT I'M ALL

ABOUT

LOVE I CAN LIVE WITHOUT

BEING HAPPY LOOKING IN

DOUBT

69

GRAVEYARD HUMER

DEATH IS ALL THE RAGE

LOVE OF BLOOD IS THE RUMER

70

THE DOOMED ALIVE AND

INTAMED

WITH FEAR CONSUMED THERE

HEARTS CUT WITH EVIL

NO AMOUNT OF LOVE CAN

HEAL THE WOUND

71

TO THE GOTHIC THE SON WILL SURRENDER

SON WILL SURRENDER

A CHILDHOOD FULL OF

THE MACABRE I REMEMBER

72

THE SEED OF MADNESS PLANTED
SHALLOW AND DEEP
AT MADNESS I LAUGH FOR
MADNESS I WEEP
MADNESS STARTED IN MY
CHILDHOOD AND ENDED IN MY
SLEEP

73

DEATH NEVER SWALLOWED ME
YOUNG
AROUND MY NECK IT HAS ALWAYS
HUNG
DEATH HAS ALWAYS BEEN MY FRIEND
WITH A SMILE I SHALL WATCH
IT COME

74

FROM LACK OF
CREATIVITY I AM
NEVER STARVING
FROM THE ROCK AND
WOOD OF CREATIVITY I AM
ALWAYS CARVING

75

AFFECTION SHREADED
LOVE DREADED
ON THE STORM OF HOPE
IT'S DEATH THAT KEEPS ME
STEADED

76

NEVERENDING SORROW

HELL TODAY DEATH TOMORROW

IN PAIN I WALLOW

THE ANGEL OF DEATH

I FOLLOW

77

I CAN'T TAKE AWAY

YOUR PAIN

I'M JUST A MAD POET

STANDING IN THE RAIN

I CAN'T GIVE YOU SHELTER

FROM THE INSANE

I'M JUST A POET

AND SELF DESTRUCTION IS

MY GAME

78

MADE OUT OF SAND
MADE OUT OF STONE
CAN'T WAIT FOR ALL OF YOU
TO LEAVE ME ALONE
I'VE GOT A REAL CONNECTION
WITH REJECTION

79

I DO LESS GOOD AND
MORE WRONG
SOME WOULD SAY
HELL IS WHERE I COME FROM
AND HELL IS WHERE I
BELONG

80

AT THE FUTURE I

SCREAM

TO DIE A GOD I DREAM

81

FROM LOVE I HIDE

SOMETIMES I THINK IT

WOULD BE EASIER TO DIE

82

FOR NADIA

YOU DRAGGED LOVE OUT OF ME

SHOWED ME HOW HAPPY I CAN

BE

YOU LOCKED THE COLD AWAY

SET THE RAINBOWS FREE

83

DON'T NEED YOU JUST NEED
MYSELF
BEING IN LOVE IS BAD FOR
MY HEALTH

I LOVE ROCK N ROLL
I'M JUST THE DEVIL
AT THE END OF THE BAR
AND I'M GOING TO EAT
YOUR SOUL

84
POEM FOR NADIA

FRIEND FOR LIFE

HELPS WITH MY TROUBLES

AND STRIFE

FOR ME HER HEART IS

OPEN WIDE

SO MUCH LOVE INSIDE

FROM EACH OTHER

THERE'S NOTHING WE HIDE

THE DAY WE MET

UNHAPPINESS DIED

85

LET THE DARKNESS
SHINE ON ME
AND SET THE DEMONS
FREE

86

I'M JUST A WORLD SHAKER
BEST FRIENDS WITH THE
UNDERTAKER
A HEARTBREAKER
HARDWORK FAKER
SUNSHINE HATER

87

WANT TO BUILD A TEMPLE
DEDICATED TO PAIN
WANT LOVE TO GO UP IN
FLAMES

88

SHE SAYS HE'S DEAD

AND FROM THE ROOM

THE DEVIL FLED

AND NOW TO HELL HE'S

FOREVER WED

89

FRIEND TO FEAR

DEATH IS ALWAYS NEAR

YOU SCREAM BUT NO ONE

HEARS

ONE LAST DREAM

ONE LAST TEAR

90

THE BEAST OF CREATIVITY

RENTS OUT MY SOUL

MADNESS OUT OF CONTROL

91

I DON'T HIDE FROM PAIN

I WANT TO GET BORNED BY

SORROWS FLAME

I GOT NO CONNECTION WITH

LOVES REFLECTION

AND YOUR LOVE WILL BREAK DOWN

THE WALLS THAT SURROUND

MY HEART

FROM YOUR LOVING SHADOW

I DON'T WANT TO PART

92

I WILL WRITE YOU A POEM
ABOUT HOW IT'S HARD TO STAY
STRONG
I WILL SING YOU A SONG
ABOUT HOW I DON'T BELONG
I WILL WRITE YOU A BOOK
ABOUT ALL THE THINGS I'VE
DONE WRONG
I WILL GIVE YOU A SPEECH
ABOUT HOW PEOPLE HATE
WHERE MY SOUL COMES
FROM

93

UNHOLY LAND
THE DARKNESS I COMMAND
YOUR BLOOD I DEMAND

94

YOU CAN DEPEND ON THE

END

DEAD FRIEND HOW AND WHEN

AND WHY DID WE PRETEND

95

DEVIL COMING AROUND THE

BEND

GOD HAS NEVER BEEN MY

FRIEND

FROM BIRTH JUST WAITING

FOR THE END

96

LOST FRIEND CRYING OUT

FOR THE END

WINTER LOVER ON YOU I

CAN ALWAYS DEPEND

97

JUST LET ME DIE ALONE

JUST LET ME DIE UNKNOWN

98

CAN'T GET DEATH OF MY MIND

PAIN ACCEPTED LOVE DECLINED

FACING BEAUTY I

WILL ALWAYS BE BLIND

99

DEATH IS MY ONLY

ESCAPE

LOVE IS PAIN

AND FRIENDSHIP IS FAKE

IN THE MORNING I DON'T

WANT TO BE AWAKE

USE YOUR ILLUSION

FRIEND OF CONFUSION

OBLIVION IS THE ONLY

SOLUTION

100

OUTSIDER THE GAP

BETWEEN LOVE AND HATE

IS GETTING WIDER

101

LOVE SICK MISERY IS

MY SIDEKICK

THE WOUNDS OF REGRET

I LICK

THE DEMONS OF

ROMANCE I WHIP

102

DEATH COME OUT TO PLAY

DEATH IS MY SHADOW

ALL NIGHT AND ALL OF

THE DAY

FOR DEATH I HOPE AND

PREY

103

ANOTHER CRUSHING DEFEAT
MY HEART SKIPPED A BEAT
ONLY HELL BELOW MY
FEET
OUT LOOKING FOR LOVE
ONLY PAIN I MEET

104

MY HEART IT POUNDS TO
A DIFFERENT BEAT
I'M TRIPPING OVER SADNESS
JUST WACKING DOWN THE
STREET
MY PARTNER IN CRIME
IS DEFEAT
MISTAKES I ALWAYS
REPEAT
AT THE GAME OF LOVE
I ALWAYS CHEAT

105

FEELING LOW
PAIN COMES FAST LOVE
MOVES SLOW
THINKING LESS ABOUT I
WANT TO STAY AND
MORE ABOUT I WANT TO
GO
SO MUCH LOVE I WILL
NEVER GET TO SHOW

106

BORN UNCLEAN
ABOUT HELL I DREAM
I SMILE YOU SCREAM
ON GOD I AIN'T KEEN
NO SUPRISES ON WHERE I'VE
BEEN

107

SELF MADE DECAY

ON THE ROAD OF HAPPINESS

I'VE LOST MY WAY

108

SICK IN THE HEAD

WE HATE EACH OTHER

BUT EVERY NIGHT AND EVERY

MORNING WERE IN THE SAME BED

MAYBE ONE DAY THAT'S

WHERE YOU'LL FIND US DEAD

109

LOVE HAS IT'S OWN GRAVEYARD

BUT ME I'M PERMANENTLY BARRED

110

FRIEND OF PAIN

GOING AGAINST THE GRAIN

ABOUT THE DAYLIGHT I

COMPLAIN

111

CAN'T BELIEVE I'M STILL

ALIVE DEATH HELPS

ME SURVIVE

INTO THE SEA OF PAIN

I DIVE

FOR LOVE I NEVER CRY

112

POEM DEDICATED TO PAIN

THROW LOVE ONTO THE FIRE

PAIN IS MY ONLY DESIRE

FROM LOVE THERE'S NOTHING

TO GAIN

MAYBE I WILL SLIT MY OWN THROAT

AND LEAVE YOU WITH THE PAIN

AM I GOINF INSANE

BLOOD SPLATERS OBSESSED BY

DISASTERS WHO TOLD YOU

LOVE MATTERS

IT'S ONLY PAIN I'M AFTER

113

ANOTHER REASON TO DIE

LOVE WON'T SAVE ME SO

DON'T EVEN TRY

ANOTHER REASON TO CRY

ONLY YOU KNOW THE REASON WHY

114

DEATH IS ALL I NEED

I STABBED LOVE

AND WATCHED IT BLEED

115

LOVE CAN GROW LIKE A

FLOWER

LOVE CAN FALL LIKE A

ROCK

LOVE CAN NEVER GET STARTED

AND LOVE CAN NEVER STOP

116

STAY DARK BLACK HEART

DOOMSDAY MARCH

TOLD YOU I NEVER LOVED

YOU RIGHT FROM THE

START

117

DIEING MIND NO MERCY

ONLY EVIL YOU WILL FIND

INSIDE

FROM MADNESS I SHALL

NEVER HIDE

118

LOVER OF TERROR

MADNESS AND TORTURE

IN BED TOGETHER

HOLY RITUALS CURSED BY THE

WORD NEVER

119
THE ROOM THAT HOLDS
EVIL I NEVER ENTER BLIND
FROM A CHILD I HAVE
BEEN OUT OF MY MIND
AND OUT OF TIME

120
AWAKEN THE HELL DEVILS
MONSTER AND TRUEST DISCIPLE
A TRUE BELIEVER I HAVE NO
RIVIL THERE CAN BE NO DENIAL

121
THE CRUEL CREATOR
LOVE HATER SOUL TAKER
A THOUSAND NIGHTMARES
THE FALL OF GOD I WAS
A TRAITOR

122

SHOW YOUR PAIN
LOOK INTO THE EYES OF
THE INSANE
WHY I'M MAD I MUST
WITH JOY EXPLAIN

123

SHE LEARNS THE BLACK
ARTS FAST DAY BY DAY
FROM LOVE WE FAST
DARK FUTURE SPELLS ARE
CAST WE WHERE NO MASK

124

THE DANCE OF THE
DEMONS A GAME PLAYED
ONLY WITH UNHOLY FEELINGS
HIDDEN MEANINGS
OF HELL I'M DREAMING

125

DARK INTRUDER VISITS THE
SUMMER HEARTS
AND ONE BY ONE LOVE
DEPARTS
NOW LIFE IS MADE OF ONLY
UNHOLY PARTS

126

USE LOVE TO WIN THE WAR
MANY TIMES I HAVE CRIED
AND ASKED WHAT DOES IT
ALL MEAN AND WHAT IS IT
ALL FOR

127

HACK OUT LOVE
BRING DESTRUCTION
UNDER THE SPELL OF
SEDUCTION
LONELINESS AND SORROW
WILL RULE TOMORROW

128

TO THE WILDERNESS FLEAS

THE COWARD

I COULD HAVE LOVED BUT WITH

HATE I WAS EMPOWERED

A CRUSHING DEFEAT

ALL ALONE WITH DEATH I

MEET

129

LOVER OF THE BLACK ARTS

LOVE TORN APART

I HAVE DESTROYED ALL THE

GOOD IN ME

I WAS BORN WITH

BUT

SHALL NOT DIE WITH

A GOOD HEART

130

TRAVELING FEAR

ALL TERRORS I WANT

KEPT NEAR

FROM CHILDHOOD FROM THE

DARKSIDE I HAVE NOT STAYED

CLEAR

131

HACK OUT THE LOVE

BRING DESTRUCTION

UNDER THE SPELL OF

SEDUCTION

LONELINESS AND SORROW

SHALL RULE TOMORROW

132

EVIL THAT HAS NO

GRAVE

DARK FORCES KEEP ME

SAFE

FROM HELL I AM

TRULY MADE

133

SHOW YOUR PAIN

LOOK INTO THE EYES OF

THE INSANE

WHY I'M MAD I MUST

WITH JOY EXPLAIN

134

DRIPPING BLOOD INSPIRES

MY CREATIVE SIDE

FROM PURE EVIL I NEVER

HIDE LONG AFTER I'ME

DEAD

THE EYES OF HORROR WILL

BE OPEN WIDE

135

MARRIED TO MADNESS

WHAT MAKES US SMILE

BRINGS YOU SADNESS

YOU WALK IN SUMMERS LOVE

WE WALK IN WINTERS

TWISTED DARKNESS

136

HORRIFYING HUMANITY

WITH PURE INSANITY

FROM BIRTH TO DEATH

ALL OF YOU I PITY

137

EXTREAM CRUELTY I GAVE YOU

A LIFE SENTENCE

MINDGAMES MADE OF PURE

HELL WERE RELENTLESS

Milton Keynes UK
Ingram Content Group UK Ltd.
UKHW022132160823
426999UK00005B/91